NOTE FROM THE PUB

Welcome to the 53rd issue of Ibbetson Street. On the front and back covers you will see the elegant artwork of Julia Kanno. Kanno has had her artwork in previous issues of *Ibbetson Street*. We are also proud to announce that Harris Gardner, our poetry editor, has been selected by the New England Poetry Club for the Sam Cornish Award. Harris' poetry and his many contributions to the Boston poetry scene were celebrated on June 25th at the Longfellow House, as part of the New England Poetry Club Summer Reading Series. In this issue we are proud to have poetry from Krikor der Hovanessian, Gary Metras, Hilary Sallick, Tomas O'Leary, Mary Buchinger, Michael Casey, Danielle Legros Georges, Charles Coe, Timothy Gager, Brendan Galvin and many others.

We would like to thank Harris Gardner, our poetry editor, and our managing editor, Lawrence Kessenich, for putting this issue together, and Steve Glines for his design work.

The Ibbetson Street Press/Endicott College Young Writers Series has released a new book of poetry by the talented undergraduate Sydney Leclerc, *Balancing Act*. This is just one of the great books we've published by students in the last decade.

I want to thank Endicott College for their continued support. Professors Dan Sklar, Mark Herlihy, and Sam Alexander are stalwart supporters of our magazine—and we applaud them for their help.

—Doug Holder, June, 2023

Ibbetson Street Press
25 School Street
Somerville, MA 02143

Publisher: Doug Holder
Managing Editors: Lawrence Kessenich, Ravi Yelamanchili
Poetry Editor: Harris Gardner
Consulting Editor: Robert K. Johnson
Art Editor: Julia Kanno
Art Consultant: Richard Wilhelm
Designer: Steve Glines
Website Manager: Steve Glines
Cover art, front and back, by Julia Kanno

Boston Area Small Press and Poetry Scene: http://dougholder.blogspot.com
Doug Holder's CV: http://dougholderresume.blogspot.com
Ibbetson Street Press: http://ibbetsonpress.com
ISCS PRESS: http://www.iscspress.com
Ibbetson Street Press Online Bookstore: http://www.tinyurl.com/3x6rgv3

ISBN 978-1-312-29989-4

The Ibbetson Street Press is supported by and formally affiliated with Endicott College, Beverly, Massachusetts. http://www.endicott.edu

No simultaneous submissions; no poems previously published in print or online. All submissions must be sent by email only to tapestryofvoices@yahoo.com—as an attachment or pasted into the body of the email.

Copyright June 2023 Ibbetson Street Press

Advertise with the Boston Area Small Press and Poetry Scene! http://tinyurl.com/ddjcal

CONTENTS

BREAKING THE RECORD 1
    Jessie Brown

IN HUGHENDEN MANOR 2
    Deborah Leipziger

NO DIRECTION, HOME 3
    Laura Cherry

LANDMEN 4
    Sydney Doyle

WINTER PREDAWN RITES 5
    Justin Hunt

REVERENCE 5
    Ruth Chad

ON A SPRING MORNING LIKE THIS 6
    Mary Buchinger

ALONG THE CONTOOCOOK - SEPTEMBER 6
    Lainie Senechal

AFTER SWIMMING AT WALDEN POND 7
    Triona McMorrow

AT JACK KEROUAC'S GRAVE ON THE DAY QUEEN ELIZABETH DIED 7
    Ruth Hoberman

OSCAR WILDE BRINGS FLOWERS TO HIS WIFE'S GRAVE 8
    Gary Metras

GOOD NIGHT 9
    Richard Hoffman

MY SOFA BECOMES A TIME MACHINE 10
    Madeleine Fuchs Holzer

ABSENCE 11
    Harris Gardner

SOLSTICE: FIFTEEN HOURS,
EIGHTEEN MINUTES OF DAYLIGHT 12
    Jacquelyn Malone

I WANT TO BE A MOTH 12
    Eileen McCluskey

BENT 13
    Chad Parenteau

She's often still with me 13
    Marge Piercy

SUCCESSION 14
    Gayle Roby

IF I WERE GOD 15
    Susan Lloyd McGarry

BEGINNING WITH A HILLTOP CEMETERY 16
    David P. Miller

12.13% 17
    Lawrence Kessenich

PURGATORY ROAD 18
    Charles Coe

FORTUNE 19
    Kathleen Aguero

TWO DREAMS PERHAPS CONNECTED 20
    Bill Tremblay

FOUR SIGNS 21
    Ted Kooser

ON WINNING A YEAR'S WORTH OF DONUTS 22
    Michael Brosnan

DISTRESS CALL FROM CONSTELLATION CANCER 23
    Tom Holmes

FIGMENTATION 24
    Wendell Smith

HOME HEALTH SUPPORT 25
    Paula Reed Nancarrow

JOURNEY 26
    Stephen M. Honig

THEY ARE LEAVING US NOW 27
    Michael Ansara

ATLAS TAKES THE STAIRS 28
    Laura Cherry

23rd 28
    Andy Hoffman

dream 28
    Danielle Legros Georges

AN AGED WIDOWER 28
    Robert K. Johnson

FOR THE LOVE OF TRAINS 29
    Ellaraine Lockie

LOOKING UP FROM ROCKY FLATS 30
    Tomas O'Leary

SPRING CHORUS 30
    Sandra Thaxter

MISGUIDED-YOSEMITE 31
    Elizabeth A. Rodgers

ONE SQUARE INCH OF SILENCE 32
    Molly Mattfield Bennett

ADOLESCENTS AND THE RIVER ROPE 33
    Bridget Seley Galway

PADMA, THE SEVENTH-BORN 34
    Denise Provost

BOTTLE TREE 34
    Deborah Leipziger

FIREWORKS 35
    Patricia L. Hamilton

For Jana; or, I remember when I wasn't even 36
    Jeff Tigchelaar

FOR I WILL CONSIDER MY CAT 37
    Dori Hale

HORIZON 38
    Jennifer Barber

HOLE-SUM 38
    Keith Tornheim

THE GLASS HARMONICA 38
    Ruth Holzer

RECIPE *STUPID* MEN COOK TO CAPTURE WOMEN 39
    Timothy Gager

LIKE FANCY PROPERTY: TANGIER #39 40
    Nina Rubenstein Alonso

BANDAGES 41
    Gloria Mindock

ONSET 42
    Karen Klein

AFFLATUS 43
    Livingston Rossmoor

CONVERSATION 44
    Krikor Der Hohannesian

THE NEIGHBORS 45
    Paulette Demers Turco

THE THEFT 46
    Ellen Austin-Li

ANYTHNG REMEMBERED IS EVENTUALLY POETRY 47
    Hilary Sallick

LAMBERTVILLE 48
    Carla Schwartz

THOSE BACKDROP CITIES 49
    Brendan Galvin

GANG WAR 50
    Zvi A. Sesling

THE ENGRAVER 51
    Michael Todd Steffen

WRITE AN ARS POETICA 52
    Molly Lynn Watt

sign-in sheets 53
    Michael Casey

THE DOG THAT RUNS THROUGH ROUGH WATERS 54
    Ryan Clinesmith

UPON READING CHRISTOPER MARLOWE'S MASSACRE IN PARIS 56
    Dennis Daly

WRITERS' BIOS 57

BREAKING THE RECORD

1. Afternoon

The sun makes a fierce glitter of the lace curtain,
slaps its fat stroke against the hot boards of the floor.
Open the door, and the white sky drops down.
The heat drapes itself around you.
It is the breath of a giant animal approaching;
it stops you full.
A toxin, slow and cruel.

2. Dreams

The storefront's packed with mannequins.
You are longing for the dark boy
who works the hot clothes press.
The train screams behind you as you run.
You are Gretel at the witch's oven.

3. The Gauze Dress

Sitting on the edge of the blue bed with
the warm wind moving
the curtains and my dress, I might as well
be naked, the way it feathers the skin,
the way it lulls. No hurry.
I might as well stand
open before the open window,
light as the birds chittering below.
It is this gentle, this inviting — the wind
hours before its hot freight
makes the leaves in the garden close,
and the insects fall silent.

—*Jessie Brown*

IN HUGHENDEN MANOR
Home of Prime Minister Benjamin Disraeli

Fig and passion fruit
vines climb the warm garden walls.
Pears redden brick.

August bees hover,
Pink roses in the parterre
Swan topiary.

Greeted by Byron,
gifts from Queen Victoria,
Disraeli's books locked.

My questions linger.
How do you make a death mask?
Out of what? Marble?

Buried in the church yard,
where a wedding just held,
hydrangea bouquet.

A summer Sunday
in ivy sun-filled stables
eating scones and cream

with black currant jam,
silver tea pot with Earl Gray,
demerara sugar.

Wisteria climbs
over History's manor
guarding us.

—*Deborah Leipziger*

NO DIRECTION, HOME

Whenever I read one of those shelter mags
        about the affluent and their fancy houses,

lush gardens, awe-inspiring water views,
        I think: but do they actually *live* there? By which

I mean, do they chop carrots on the sustainably
        sourced marble, nap on the modern

upholstered chaise, wrangle a Labradoodle
        on the Oushak rug, sway

in the gazebo swing with a blueberry muffin
        and coffee and nowhere to be but here?

That's what I would envy, if I imagined
        it were true. I bring my cup to the couch

and look for just a moment at the trees,
        swathed in green or naked as nymphs,

before I pick up my phone or laptop
        or remote. Sometimes a cat joins me.

It's hard to be anywhere, but while I'm here
        I'll keep trying to live here.

—Laura Cherry

LANDMEN

Still, when the oil and gas men came,
we prayed for a drill.

We'd be paid by the acre.
Woke weekdays at cockcrow to lean in
cold mornings at town hall listening
to lowball offers whispered
like lottery numbers.

For months we waited
with crossed fingers.
Hope is a labor
and I want to say ours
meant we loved the land.

We planted vegetables:
cucumbers, onions, tomatoes,
bell peppers, heads of lettuce.
Our soil a constellation
of fertilizer. In spring, we circled
saplings in chicken-wire,
watered them at sundown.
We filled buckets with wild raspberries,
thin as thimbles and hairless—nothing
like the kind sold in the grocery.

We dug a pond and filled it with fish.
The turtles came. The ducks
laid eggs. Our hands shooed away dangers
from the nests. Sentimental,
even though we knew we shouldn't
get involved. We were involved
with the bramble, the creek,
the wriggling things beneath a turned
over stone.

But when it turned
out nothing was under our little plots
except last season's cold bulbs
and talks at town hall dwindled into nothing
but wasted mornings piled up like leaves,
we skimmed the surface
of our hope and trundled home
to dirt and rock. The water in the pond—
not yet iced over—clear
as a blank check.

—*Sydney Doyle*

WINTER PREDAWN RITES

More than fifty years have passed,
but snow still blanks our yard, and ice
chokes our windows. My sister and I
elbow in the hall, fight for first rights
to the bathroom. In the kitchen,
our mother clangs up breakfast,
frets we'll be late. Our father leaps
from bed and shaves, ear bent to KFH
and Bruce Behymer's stockyard report—
the prices of wheat and corn, barley,
milo and oats, the latest quotes
for cattle, sheep and hogs an incantation
riding the hot breath of our furnace,
the warm-up clicks of cold metal ducts.

Don't ask what it meant, or where
it went. I'm still lugging north to school
against a stiff, sunup wind—
along those mud streets, those frozen ruts.

—*Justin Hunt*

REVERENCE

Rain gathered
in a white vase

I left out after watering
garnet pansies,

rain that flowed
over maple, lilac, andromeda—

a heady scent—

I will save this water,
alchemy of cloud and mist

cool harvest of sky
for the next dry blooms,

hear its music spill back into black earth,
a balm for my sadness.

—*Ruth Chad*

ON A SPRING MORNING LIKE THIS

  when the air is soft
holding afternoon's rain
and the sun comes filtered down
on muted green moss
unfurling from a rotted stump
  I stop on the city sidewalk
and peer into the fence
looking for my childhood
it should be there new again
nourishing formless tender

—*Mary Buchinger*

ALONG THE CONTOOCOOK - SEPTEMBER

The weather wavers towards summer
on a warm sultry breeze.
With the windows wide open,
a chorus of night sounds:
crickets chirp in a percussive choir,
owls hoot from the nearby forest,
wind whispers in the trees,
tears of rain tiptoe on the ground
and gently shake the river's reeds.
At dawn thoughts of autumn return
as the early sun reflects
off the changing colors of leaves.

—*Lainie Senechal*

AFTER SWIMMING AT WALDEN POND

I think of that pond now, the day we saw it,
within the trees, cool even in summer sun.

I vowed then to stay aware of wildness,
nourish it when I got home, not to forget.

A man could build his own house
As naturally as a bird builds its nest.

It's easy to think like Thoreau, as spring comes,
to romance about building a house in a wood.

Although some say he wasn't really honest,
that his mother brought his dinner every day.

—Triona McMorrow

AT JACK KEROUAC'S GRAVE ON THE DAY QUEEN ELIZABETH DIED

What beautiful weather! I said, but really, the sun was scathing—
it had licked the Canadian Club bottle dry and robbed the Woodbridge red
of any hint of redemption. An avid, shoddy scene: beer cans
hunched in a litter of ballpoint pens. We weren't sure

why we'd come—two oldsters with appointments to keep—
and panicked when an endless chain of cars blocked the way out.
Do you think all this does anything for the dead? you asked,
as cars inched and idled at the gate, in each a profile solemn

as the queen's on coins. *It's for the living,* I said. Why did I feel bereft—
here in this cemetery with no one special to mourn, devoid of wounds,
tattoos, stupidities, grief: a stone without a grave to lie upon. *What I don't get,*
I said, *is why leave whisky for a man who died of drink?*

That's when on my phone I saw the queen had died. Already
crowds were leaving flowers, ecstatic with grief.

—Ruth Hoberman

OSCAR WILDE BRINGS FLOWERS TO HIS WIFE'S GRAVE

The sea had no sparkle on Oscar Wilde's
last trip to Genoa, and the sun hesitated
over the greedy horizon. First lunch, tasteless,

mechanical, the wine even worse. Then
the cemetery. He lingered before a marble cross
and touched his wife's carved name.

He carried flowers.
What else could he bring her in death
that he hadn't in life.

The surrounding hills, soft, delicate,
a token of early spring.
The shock of her name divorced from his:

>   Constance Mary
>   daughter of
>   Horace Lloyd

as if Oscar never was, marriage a sham,
mere convention to a phobic public. Yet here
he stood in the garden of her resting,

muttering to himself, *the uselessness
of regret.* He wasn't thinking about
the money problems her death

would cause; that came later,
when he wrote, *sunlight is half
my income.* He didn't think about

his sons in London he'd never see again.
He placed the flowers by the stone
and prayed that she knew he loved her also.

—*Gary Metras*

GOOD NIGHT
contra Dylan Thomas

Go gently now, my father, your work is done.
The main things, the important things, you did.
Let peace be what you, old champion, have won.

Think of how serenely a shadow when the sun
goes down becomes the night where it is hid.
Go now, my father, gently, your work is done.

Go. I'll stay and be the sad and angry one
who thinks of your afflictions and grows livid.
Let peace be what you, old laborer, have won

from bosses and creditors; let any confusion
be ours, and you be finished with it, lucid.
Go, my father, gently now, your work is done.

Regrets, repairs, resentments, things undone,
those several past due bills are no longer valid.
Let peace be what you, tired oarsman, have won,

no need now to row, no need to be anyone,
as waves calm to swells and swells fall placid.
Gently, my father, go now, your work is done.
Let peace at long last be what you have won.

—Richard Hoffman

MY SOFA BECOMES A TIME MACHINE

The cat jumps in my father's lap.
He pets her, says, "Hortontown.
"I worked summers
on Phineas Horton's farm."

And my father is fourteen
in hayfields, raising the blade
of the mower, riding
the horse drawn cart.

To earn needed wages,
he is in the barn,
watching tongs lift bales
to the loft for winter.

His work finished, he trots
over to see the housekeeper,
for another long talk
on her porch at the big house.

I wonder what she says
to him, the tall thin boy
with dark eyes who prayed
with *tefillin* each morning.

And what he says to her,
this country woman
with graying blond hair,

who owns two cats,
one Persian, one Angora,
and had never seen a Jew.

—*Madeleine Fuchs Holzer*

ABSENCE

The tale of the prodigal son
Is so old and often told, but
It never becomes a stale lesson.

A profligate child named Judah, leaves to wander,
Unwary and adrift in an adverse world,
Then returns home with depleted pockets.

Empty of hope, he arrives at his parents' door.
A feast greets him with no rebukes for dessert,
While industrious siblings are sidelined

With adhesive smiles adhering to cryptic faces.
Their moral minds would suggest that he should
Have pursued a more prolonged itinerary.

What if he had followed their taciturn advice?
Relief would have been replaced by the angst
Of absence. The family picture would be minus one,

The empty spot palpable. Some hearts, but
Not all, would overflow with want,
The poignant grief for the missing son

Who disappeared into a pernicious sea
Of roiling humanity; the present reality
Keeps those abrasive thoughts at bay.

—*Harris Gardner*

SOLSTICE: FIFTEEN HOURS, EIGHTEEN MINUTES OF DAYLIGHT

It's never enough, so in defeat
the hard-shouldered sun slams
into the lake and, glancing, rams itself
under a grove of trees.
Backlit by the flight of light
even the poison ivy glows—
devil in a fop's clothes.
Night lurks in the shadows.

Light worries the top edge
of sedge into a fringed sheen.
Underneath, fetid roots hide
in the deepening green
where the water sours
and dead creatures catch in the reeds.
Night lurks in the shadows.

Across the lake cars glitter
through breaks in trees. Light
in rapid transit. Light
in the v-wakes the geese make,
in the slapping lap of waves,
in ripples—like a spill of chill
across the water.
Night lurks in the shadows.

—*Jacquelyn Malone*

I WANT TO BE A MOTH

The moths flap at my door,
all slap-happy pre-determination,

pale wings like parchment
on which no words are written.
I want to flutter

too, live briefly, even stupidly
and only because

it cannot be helped.

Like them, I will obey
elemental idiocies, another
flimsy simpleton

unspooling my nearly-nothing life,
barely mattering

and off we'll go,
our kite bodies
crackling, crackling.

—*Eileen McCluskey*

BENT
For Charles Simic

Silence finally
cannibalized,
they let you lie.

Warmongers know
both soldiers
and victims
deserve final rest.

Stay in ground,
wait for next
hapless bastard

who no longer
tries to solve
riddle of how
to lift self into sky

by way of tugging
on bootstraps. Instead
he'll stare down

as if he can meet
your eyeless gaze
through the strata
of mass grave soil.

—*Chad Parenteau*

She's often still with me

I'm the age we thought you were
when you died of stroke, Father
leaving you on the floor passed
out while he picked up every shred

of glass from the lamb that broke
when you fell with a cry. You
had no birth certificate, so your
age was one of your mysteries.

I died last October but the rescue
squad revived me into my new
life, more fragile, now wide open
to each moment drab or shining.

He is never with me. No love lost
there. But you haunt my dreams,
have molded my aging face to
yours in the mirror. I'm my own

woman but also always permanently
your daughter till the end.

—*Marge Piercy*

SUCCESSION

1. "The king is dead. Long live the king."
   One lies in state; the next takes the throne
   with pomp and circumstance, glasses raised.
   The hungry forage for scraps of food.

2. Most mothers and fathers want more
   for their child than they had growing up—
   to avoid the pox, make friends, keep safe
   from bullies, know their parents' love.

3. Beside our back door, irises grow,
   bloom midnight-blue on tall thin stalks.
   As the bloom wilts, below it a bud
   rises through the wrinkled petals.

4. With care, a monarch chooses a milkweed,
   then the leaf to bear her egg. She won't live
   to see it hatch, a striped caterpillar
   that will eat its home, spin a cocoon,
   transform   emerge   fly.

—*Gayle Roby*

If I were God

we would all be birds.
Some of us would stay at home,
never leaving our acre, but most
would fly and fly twice a year
to and from the warm,
often together, like the geese,
keeping the pattern
and taking turns to lead.

Some of us would eat worms and
grubs, some berries and nuts,
some would pick at carcasses.
We would nest, invite each other in
and some would go and others
would not. Some of us would mate
for life, and some would skitter-scatter
through each chance encounter.

Most of us would fall of exhaustion
and be a meal for something as we
came back to the earth.
Some would be plucked
out of the sky or from a branch
or at the water's edge. I mean
we would still suffer and die.

But we would rise each
morning, singing the sun
up, each evening
singing it down, except
for those of us who
traveled through the
home of night.

We would still be of this world
and live and die by its rhythms.
But none of us,
singly or together, would
inflict great harm.

—*Susan Lloyd McGarry*

BEGINNING WITH A HILLTOP CEMETERY

Please, I tell myself, attention. My grandparents'
headstone in summer. Don't look on its lichen
as given. Be alert for a strong fallen twig
to scrape the gouges of names and years.
It's a long forgetfulness between hushed visits.

Please, although I extend as far back
as their deep lines, I must not then fail
forward. I could repeat *You have this time,
it's nearly done*. But don't be another man
so very clenched behind his breastbone. No.
Now at this café window, with all the voices
and espresso-steam hiss, set my eyes
ahead for a long look outward:

Grey sky, don't drench this student as she carries
a bag of dinner. Please, late season snow,
slide from the windshields. Let there be crocus
on her fingers, lilac along the solo walk to her room.

For if I'm one to clean gravestones in shade,
I must also be one to watch these footsteps
through the slush. I may not ignore
their flinches in sleet. Be awake to their
instrument cases and heavy packs.
What can I give them that isn't asleep?

—*David P. Miller*

12.13%

It's official: that's how Jewish I am.
My sister sussed it out through genealogy.
I'd long thought we were purely German—
even in the New World, our Germans married
other Germans on rich Wisconsin farms.

But it turns out, if my family had stayed
in the Fatherland, we would have been outcasts
not Nazis. This is a great relief. I hate Nazis.
And it turns out they would have hated me.
Better dead than red and white and black.

I once considered converting to Judaism. Who
(besides Nazis) could help admiring such a religion?
People oppressed for millennia still giving
to the communities they live in—to charities, arts,
social programs—instead of sequestering themselves.

I became a Quaker, instead, but I will always admire
Jews, always be proud of my 12.13%. If only we
could all learn from our suffering as Jews have, identify
with others who have suffered and relieve their suffering—
even if we only did it 12.13% of the time.

—Lawrence Kessenich

PURGATORY ROAD

We were told in Parochial school that Purgatory was the place for souls not damned to Hell, but needed purification before ascending to Heaven, souls guilty of unconfessed venial, not mortal sins. There was fire and suffering in Purgatory, but just for a while. How long a while was not explained. But we were told that if you died before you confessed your venial sins the chances would pretty good you'd wind up in Purgatory.

Purgatory wasn't like Hell where the damned burned for all eternity. As grade school kids, the concept of eternity was somewhat unclear. But one day Sister Helen explained eternity by telling us to imagine a solid brass globe, the size of the Earth. Once every thousand years, a dove flies by and brushes the globe with the tip of a wing. The time it would take that touch to wear the brass globe to nothing is just the first second of eternity. Sister Helen scanned our small, perplexed brown faces and nodded, confident her explanation had gotten her point across.

My main takeaway was that that even if Purgatory was a drag, it was better than Hell. At least you eventually got sprung. I thought of Purgatory as Heaven's Waiting Room, like the doctor's office, tables piled with ancient copies of "Reader's Digest" and "Life Magazine" and "Highlights for Children." Only with fire. Of course, I wasn't foolish enough to share any of these speculations with the nuns or priests. We weren't allowed to question matters of theology.

The rites and rituals of youth, the mysterious incantations in a secret and ancient language, the calm, inflexible certainties of the Baltimore Catechism, the dark and quiet confessional box, are all dust-covered relics in my mind's closet. But one time, driving through a small New England town I passed a sign for "Purgatory Road," and the name tossed me into the Wayback Machine, to when my life was ruled by pale faces draped in black, who spoke with great assurance in the voice of God on all matters spiritual.

I think now that maybe this earthbound life is itself something like a Purgatory Road, that navigating the potholes of our sorrows and disappointments, the roadblocks of fear and failure, the endless random acts of casual cruelty, is our own rite of purification, that crucible of cold fire through which we all must pass to become ourselves.

—*Charles Coe*

FORTUNE

The fortune teller comes at me waving her arms. "Stop," she yells. "You forgot your fortune." I turn around and there it is, gathered around her, the future she told me of: the tall, dark man with the eyepatch next to my son's broken leg, trouble at work in the person of the Academic Dean glowering and talking as he runs, and the trip the fortune teller mentioned must be a jaunt to Switzerland for there's the Matterhorn jostling the Dean. My mother's illness, the small promotion, the quarrel with my husband soon mended, all are milling around. "Such carelessness," the psychic scolds. "Now you'll have to organize them all yourself. The time lines are jumbled." She disappears leaving me with a future I can't seem to control, vainly scrambling to recall the order of events she predicted. By now a crowd has gathered, traffic snarled in both directions, a police siren rushing up the street. When the officer approaches, I don't know what to tell him. *No, I don't have a parade permit.* Then we're in the squad car, all of us: my husband glaring at the tall dark man, the Dean, who has rescinded my promotion, perching uncomfortable on top of the Matterhorn, and me moaning over my poor son's leg, cradling my mother's illness in my arms, wondering if all this will lead to the event the fortune-teller couldn't quite focus in her crystal ball.

—*Kathleen Aguero*

TWO DREAMS PERHAPS CONNECTED

I fly above a forest of lodge-pole pine following
the course of a winding river toward where it
plays out on the plains. Somehow by compressing
the *chi* between my hands as if playing an invisible
accordion I am able to defeat the fiction of gravity
as I hover over a ranch where a young man shoots
tin cans off a fence. "What're you doing up there?"
he asks me. "Dreaming," I answer, strangely self-
aware. He has a pain in the neck from staring up.
"You're a good moving target," he says. I see from
the tattoos on his shaved head he means business,
so I wheeze myself over the foothills through deserts
to the ocean where I alight, exhilarated, exhausted,
from my flight to the continent's end, a long beach
on a huge ocean with black clouds. A young woman
in a business suit also stares into the oncoming storm.
"They say it's El Patron," she murmurs as a tsunami
rolls toward us. It crashes on a pier, leaving twisted
pilings. There's no damage to the beach where a large
crowd gathers. "What is this about," I ask her. She
says, "Revolution. Why don't you join us. You know
you want to." "I don't think so," I say, "I've done
that. Sorry for the spoiler, but it doesn't end well."

—*Bill Tremblay*

FOUR SIGNS

A couple of miles short of the prison
I sped past a brown sign lettered in white
reading Penitentiary Ahead. Don't Pick Up
Hitchhikers. A mile farther, another sign
like the first, and then a good quarter mile
of poured concrete wall, showing old seams
from the forms, topped with bright razor-wire
and three turrets with two motionless guards
silhouetted in each. At the far end
was an exercise yard with a ten-foot high
double fence, it too topped with razor wire,
nobody inside, just a backstop and bases
in freshly mown grass. And then it was all
swiftly behind me, no one on the shoulder
trying to look normal, thumbing a ride.
A mile farther on, I passed another sign
like the others, this time across the road
and, from the back, unpainted plywood
with a two-by-four frame for support, with
a short center board like a spine, all this,
including the two four-by-four uprights,
bleached a uniform gray. On the cross-piece
spanning the sign's base was what looked,
at a glance, like a nest, twigs and grass.
A mile farther stood another sign, again
with its unpainted back turned to me
as it shouldered ahead, showing its best face
to the traffic, nobody slowing, everyone
speeding on and the signs falling behind.

—*Ted Kooser*

ON WINNING A YEAR'S WORTH OF DONUTS

One morning, driving nowhere,
trying hard not to let the voice in my head
add another weary addendum to the plot of me,

I pulled into a donut shop parking lot,
looking for a cup of coffee as a way to inject
alacrity into the drone of time.

I can't remember what they said. Something
about me being the 100th customer — which meant,
Hey, Mr. Lucky, you've won a year's worth of donuts!

They interviewed me for a local radio program.
I said, *Wow*. I said, *Thanks*. I said, *I like donuts*.
I didn't tell them I lost my job a month earlier.

But I did remind them that on the previous day
a man with a fear-fed soul and twenty-four guns
slaughtered sixty people at a Las Vegas concert.

I pointed out that no one claimed to have seen the man
lug twenty-four guns across the hotel lobby,
into the elevator, down the hall, into his room.

No one claims to have suspected a thing
as he set up cameras, shattered windows.
To the gamblers, he was just another wanderer

navigating this desert of chance.
A radio reporter said, *Yes, sad.*
Then asked, *What's your favorite flavor?*

Every day now, I drive over for my donut.
I used to eat the whole thing and think about luck.
Was I lucky? Is this a good story?

I tell my new parking-lot pigeon friends
that we're bound to ride this tragedy for a while now,
the fear-fed kettledrumming more fear.

We will do this, I tell the attentive pigeons,
until we're done.
Or we'll wake and change.

In the early weeks, I plowed through the donut line-up —
cream-filled, powdered, glazed, dipped. Now, I only eat

half an old-fashioned, because, you know, I'm getting fat.

I collect my donut and coffee, head to the parking lot,
break the donut in half, give half to the pigeons.
When I sit on the curb, the birds pigeon-strut over,

usually three, sometimes four. They share sloppily,
but never seem to mind how things turn out.
When the half donut is gone, that's it. It's gone.

Afterward, they strut in random patterns,
then fly off to some nearby spot to watch the world.
I drink my coffee and watch them watch.

—*Michael Brosnan*

DISTRESS CALL FROM CONSTELLATION CANCER

for this desperation
there is a cure
with radiation

long after a war
I'm out there
wide as your ears

keep open your lenses
as you will today
discover alien existence

I listened in
to your telescopes
hoping for life signs

and radio waves
after my own
decades of scans

I write this to you
the day after I died
it will arrive

—*Tom Holmes*

FIGMENTATION

The Buddha sat beneath the Bo
'til nothing bored him anymore
continued sitting hatched a plan
to mitigate the pain huMAN.

The sole path to soul's success is
not through material excesses
or financially rewarded gumption,
but inconspicuous consumption.

For a happiness, which you can't measure,
try slowing your pursuits of pleasure
replace desires for what's in fashion
with great big dollops of compassion.

Eventually you will have to share
your body with the evening air
for even if it buried be
it will escape through roots of tree.

And when the body's been discarded
the soul (unless it's been retarded
by its various attachments
like a drunk who uses breath mints)
will with, Oh, what's the word? Elation?
merge with the substance of creation.

—*Wendell Smith*

HOME HEALTH SUPPORT

Not if the diagnosis is Alzheimer's.
Not if her caregiver has arthritis
and high blood pressure
and chronic kidney disease.

Not if he insists *she'll go
to a nursing home
over my dead body*
and his anger names our fears.

Not if he can't get her up
when she falls. Not if he can't
stay awake and she wanders.
Not if she can't bathe herself.

But if she shuffles and stumbles
on a walk with her son
breaks her nose
fractures both eye sockets

and there's bleeding
on the brain then alleluia
there's a code for help.
Allowable expenses include

an Occupational Therapist
and a Physical Therapist
and a Personal Care Assistant
to aid in recovery.

But what if there is
no recovery? What if
palliative care sounds
too much like end of life

to the man in charge
of less and less each day?
Then home health must wait
for another emergency.

Whose will it be?

A man's iron will breaking
his bent and questioning frame.
Fairy lights fading in the tangles
of a woman's brain.

—*Paula Reed Nancarrow*

JOURNEY

My body has dragged my mind
cushioned by hard shell and soft shock-absorbent packaging
to where I am
over decades
full of things I remember and
no doubt
things I have forgotten, for good or ill,
to bring me to this place I cannot identify
on a road to somewhere I cannot imagine.
I am happy midst all the confusion
and not apt to complain in any event.

Flowers smell a way we perceive as sweet
although they too have had their own journey.
Travelled long distances to share this moment with me
without the burden of the questions I carry
and cannot shed.
Is it their simplicity that saves them
from the sour sweat of my travels
or is it some effort of will
the knack of which has been denied me?
Seems unfair, to be beautiful and serene,
but I suppose they will fade before I do
—though come to think of it,
their heirs will decorate my grave.

—*Stephen M. Honig*

THEY ARE LEAVING US NOW

Gloria Richardson, Charles Sherrod, Bob Moses, Casey Hayden
Giant hearted, young and lightning lit,
They heard the call. Stood up,
Sat in. Marched. Organized.
John Lewis, Jane Stembridge, Unita Blackwell, Rev. C.T. Vivian
Their whole lives tender to love.
They were the flung pebbles
Whose ripples became tidal waves.
Curtis Hayes, Colia Liddell, Sam Block, Betty Garman Marsha Joyner
They taught, fought, wrote, thought,
And gave until there was little left,
Spindles unwound; sprits wounded
And yet they found the heart
To keep on keeping on.
Jim Jones, Martha White, 'Rip" Patton, Eva Partee McMillan, Jesse Morris
Each month brings the news that another has left us.
They were not giants, were desperately afraid,
But still, brave, played their parts.
Now it seems only right that at night,
The stars appear fewer, the light less,
The looming sky darker.

—*Michael Ansara*

ATLAS TAKES THE STAIRS

It's tough, to be honest,
when you're carrying what I am.
I don't mean to complain,

but it's not just climbing them,
as you'd expect; descending is
almost worse – staying balanced

without looking at my feet,
trusting the next step to be there,
and the next. And when I fall

it's spectacular – limbs pin-
wheeling in space, a gigantic
slapstick, impact resounding

as I land fully on one arm,
the other still cradling the world.

—*Laura Cherry*

23RD

    The stars and sun lead
And I follow to a meadow,
A stream, a glade:
Places that refresh me.
Sometimes, the glade
Overgrows into a forest, and I
Fear harm in every shadow –
    But then I remember:
The moon and wind
Have brought me to this
Moment: if shadows can kill me,
I must be too weak to live.
Even these seeming threats
Can strengthen and renew me.
    What brought me here saves me.
Nature embraces me like
A child, like a dying man –
And here I am always home.

—*Andy Hoffman*

dream

my feet dangle
like little birds
from the bed

my dream is
a good one
in it I tell two
women I adore
and cannot
tell apart

how it is that
things move
in my heart

they write me
the lost cities
where I once lived
insisting women
like birds can be
a problem
but this is my
dream and I decide
how to tell
the truth

—*Danielle Legros Georges*

AN AGED WIDOWER

He welcomes the scrape of his knife
as he rinses off plates at the sink,
welcomes the dishwasher's thrum
and the kettle's whistling water

ready to make him some tea,
welcomes—oh. yes—every sound
that fills the kitchen's silence
with the loud music of noise.

—*Robert K. Johnson*

FOR THE LOVE OF TRAINS

The Girl

2:00 a.m. trains became nightly lullabies to a child
when they ran a few hundred feet from her house
in a tiny Montana farm town
The faraway rumble a baritone father's voice
that carried comfort over the prairie
The whistle softened by distance into pianissimo
The slowing rhythm of clickety-clack
like the wind-down of her music box
Headlights through her window
haloed the picture of Jesus on the wall
A prayerful silent song of protection in the black of night
Then onomatopoeia of hiss and screech of brakes
as the lullaby became a poem
And reversed itself into a perfect palindrome
that emptied into the girl's deep sleep

The Wife

In Big City California baths became the woman's
bedtime ritual with bubbles, bath salts
and the distant whistle of a 10:20 p.m. Caltrain
The sound a rocking chair of nostalgia
A prescription for that deep sleep
A comfort until it became a confusion
caught between recollection and catastrophe
after her husband stepped in front of one of those Caltrains
Her husband who was also Montana-made to revere that train
The wife wonders was it like meeting an old friend
Or like walking into the arms of a first lover
Was it because Jesus no longer looks down from the wall
The whistle of that Caltrain switches tracks
between ballad, serenade and elegy
Every measure is a question

—*Ellaraine Lockie*

LOOKING UP FROM ROCKY FLATS

I hope the mountains suffer me to love them,
knowing that they're stone cold to how I feel.
Out in the free air, out on rocks and space,
those giants rising from flat earth reveal
a magnitude more dignity and grace
than humble decency ascribes oneself.
Try to imagine (for it is a trial)
that all the elements of earth respond
to all we feel or think about them. Being
a suitor of tree or shrub, or stony upgrowth
in a realm laid waste yet glorious, commands
romance as subtle as a ghost's.
Stand here, as though a whisper of yourself,
and caution all who've come along
that time, at last, is stopped and sacred.
No bargain, no reciprocation, looms.
Your life comes wrapped in moments of the world:
Its gift, as simple as yourself, is awe.

—Tomas O'Leary

SPRING CHORUS
    For Catherine Lugar

She dreamed a chorus rise of bird song,
of a spring with ev'ry branch in bloom
There burst from each a symphony of tunes.
A whistle, a twitter, an ascending trick of tongue.

The call and response, they rick-a-shay
as light, as flight and fresh freedom play,
as blossoms of dogwood or cherry
let loose their scents—a pink and purple flurry.

SIx springs have past, you are not here to know—
how busy the bees, how noisy birds' preenings glow
How life has not subsided nor dulled for your choir,
but ever more insists on all that your songs require.

—Sandra Thaxter

MISGUIDED-YOSEMITE

No good guide goes unpunished.
Our cherished Smoky the Bear
Taught us to love the forest,
To take scrupulous care with matches.
The guide now regrets
That we sewed our girl scout badges, inspired,
"Only you can prevent forest fires"

Because, unknowingly,
We extinguished the hearth
of wise forest burning,
Smothered generations of shaman-tended fire...
which cleared debris,
to let the young ones thrive.

Instead, of praising us,
the forest became angry with us.
Uncontrolled conflagrations
of sacred Sequoia
clouded the mid-day sky with wind-swept red,
and carbon spires,
enraged by our not allowing fires.

We mortals, have unlearned
how to harness fire,
and do not respectfully fear it.
It is extremely cunning, fierce, and bloodthirsty.
The lands are ravaged,
But those who live within its ken
Love its trouble and its rage,
Its romance, intrigue and drama,
And, circling in fertility and hearth,
We try again.

—*Elizabeth A. Rodgers*

ONE SQUARE INCH OF SILENCE

From enclosed worlds, some escape to the coast
where fog and incessant rain cloak fallen logs,
ferns, giant trees; there, far from daily life,
they might dream. Perhaps, somewhere
there are blazed markers to follow
on over rocks, roots and sudden streams
where one might chance upon the Square Inch
of Silence deep within a forest of old trees.
There, under drip of rain, in fog orange fungi gleam
against darkest green of fir. Within the silence
breath and heart are loud, echo of tumult; cries of birds,
of the living and dying touch the quiet of the world's forest.

*

Perhaps some dead night or break of day someone walks
Away from the city, through towns, out beyond
forgotten factories, past empty fields,

On through green air and soak of grass
past a battered pier sunk
in still water.

The trail climbs the Olympic mountains;
in the Enchanted Valley elk winter
below 10,000 waterfalls.

Now the days are short, the nights long and deep. Orion
is bright in the sky. Wanderers we are blown
by the wind we know not where.

—*Molly Mattfield Bennett*

ADOLESCENTS AND THE RIVER ROPE

We would meet at the river's edge
where the river rope hung.
Those were the days I yearned
competing with the boys.
I could not stay still in that proof.

Barefoot I climbed the slanted trunk
and grabbed the rope;
one foot sturdy on the knot
I pushed off with the other.

My hands tight and thighs squeezed
I felt the air breeze
softly through my hair
as I swung high
and let go.

Freed into the cool water.
I swam like a fish,
I could stay under for so long.

But the changing was upon me.
I felt a hand grab my ankle
then my thigh.
My stomach tingled.
My thoughts turned to kisses.
Laughing I yanked away
and swam to shore.

—Bridget Seley Galway

PADMA, THE SEVENTH-BORN

Her native city didn't suit her health.
This delicate child—fragile as a flower—
was sent to live with Auntie, near the shore.

How her mother's sister doted on her!
Like royalty, not just provided for,
but cherished, dressed in pink and turquoise silks.

Trips to the sweet shop brought delight to both.
Fed *ras malai*, the frail child grew robust;
walks in the fresh sea air soon healed her lungs.

When Auntie married, the child couldn't stay
in some unknown house, with a half-known man.
She was sent back to her crowded home.

Her far-away life, multiplied by time,
had bred a distance subtler than miles;
all siblings reevaluated roles.

Wary, she fit in. Graceful as a rose,
she understood her charms, and kept aloof—
in search of love, but always wanting proof.

—Denise Provost

BOTTLE TREE
Inspired by the sculpture "Vertical Hold"
by Nari Ward at the Museum of Modern Art

All my losses
        make me hunger
                for possession.

Fill my bottles
        with rain and desire.

Vessels held by string
        collect sap
                gather filaments,
                        brim with sunset.

I long to be filled.

—Deborah Leipziger

FIREWORKS

Born too late, I missed all those Gidget surfer movies,
watching only the Sally Field TV version in reruns.
I remember nothing but Moondoggie's name
and the furrowed brow of the widowed father
as he tried to corral his boy-crazy teen.
By the time a sequel, *Gidget Grows Up*,
aired on *Movie of the Week*, I was on the verge
of puberty, not quite interested in specific boys
but absorbing various tropes of television romance.
During Gidget's glamorous stint as a UN tour guide,
she fell for an older man. But then Moondoggie/Jeff
showed up in his crisp Air Force uniform and proposed
as brilliant Fourth-of-July fireworks filled the sky,
breathtaking night-blooms reflecting in the East River.

I never disclosed to anyone the ideal I developed
from that movie. Such notions imprint on us
without our knowing. Imagine my shock years later
when my boyfriend drove me to our local mall
on July 3 to watch an early fireworks display,
our heads craned upward as we stood surrounded
by parked cars. Enthralled by the squealing rockets
and glittery showers of light, my boyfriend—
now my husband—suddenly scrambled
to rummage in the car's glove compartment,
fumbled with a small box, and dropped to one knee,
the national anthem's blaring through the loudspeakers
signaling the show was almost over. Entranced,
I gazed at his earnest, upturned face as a sizzling
color-burst exploded behind him, dazzling, glorious.

—Patricia L. Hamilton

For Jana; or, I remember when I wasn't even

old enough to drink
legally I mean

I remember being 20 that is
and unmarried

and now
a few winks/blinks/drinks later I'm

somehow writing a 20th Anniversary Poem
I'm in my 40s and have been

wed for half my life give or take
give and take sleep and wake

to you and how are you
still there still

here with me when I can't help
but wonder if I've given you

too much
yet not enough of me

like when I finally told you
the bad part of my upbringing

or how
you handled it better than me

your cancer
have I given you

more cause to leave than to stay
when constantly I forget to remember

the certain sound you make
when you finish a book you liked

or your skill with the pen
till I stumble on one of your sketches

or the time we ran out of tortillas
during Covid so you just made your own

and maybe I pretend to hate it

when you slay me in Dr. Mario

or Scrabble or Boggle or Blitz
but I wouldn't have it

any other way
or you

and this is so
not the end

—*Jeff Tigchelaar*

FOR I WILL CONSIDER MY CAT
                after Christopher Smart

Missy Beaucoup, trouser cat, a girl
with boyish ways,
Maine Coon shag lump,
belly of sherpa fleece
sunk in a sleeping trough.

Rodent maven
at the cellar window
to study all moving things,
enemies crossing the moat-yard.
Guard cat, spook.

A crawlscape through the little door,
up twenty-seven steps in four seconds,
claw zeal for a gold glitter ball,
spigot waterfall: a drink! a drink!

At first light: many leaping events,
murmurings, whisker vibrato.

—*Dori Hale*

HORIZON
—starting with 4 Emilio Prados lines

*Today the sea appears
in gray and green stripes.
A fish jumps onto a bank.
A bird dives into the waves.*

In the distance, a trawler
wears a halo of gulls.
Who is piloting it?
Where will the voyage end?

If the horizon gulps
the red disc of the sun
and twilight sets the first
evening star alight,

will the cormorants
at the end of the dock
still hoist their wings
to dry in the salty air?

And the sandbar,
landing pad for the gulls,
when will it sink back
like a body into the night?

—Jennifer Barber

HOLE-SUM

There's ANGER in DANGER,
and DANG is there, too,
when you fall in a hole
that wasn't for you.
But someone forgot
the sign that should say
DANG there's a hole, ER,
step out of the way.

—Keith Tornheim

THE GLASS HARMONICA

Mozart's quintet (K. 617) for winds,
strings and glass harmonica
twitches your ears into spasms.

It peels paint
off the walls
of empty rooms.

Its hypnotic tones
in small doses, are thought
to have therapeutic value,

but too much will
grate on your nerves, inciting
melancholy or hysteria.

Moistened fingers rub the rims
of tuned glass bowls,
creating something like music.

If you tried this at home
with juice tumblers,
you'd get slapped.

The voice of the glass harmonica:
broken teeth
on broken ice.

Hearing the modulations
between throaty and shrill
makes you feel really weird.

An unlikely instrument—
like us, it didn't have
much of a future.

Is it here?
Is it there? It's difficult
to get a grip on it,

and you can't escape
with a glass harmonica
from a pogrom, like you can with a fiddle.

—Ruth Holzer

RECIPE *STUPID* MEN COOK TO CAPTURE WOMEN

Simmer on the future
if she wants to marry.

Re-slice negative behaviors
of her current companion, loudly,

chop them so the aroma is
impossible now to overlook.

Add wine, then reduce the quantity.
Lie if you must. Lie, a lot.

Pound about money,
what you do for work.

Then pinch some salt over
your well-seasoned apartment,

Proclaiming distaste toward,
the dirty bourgeoisie.

Don't forget the presentation, posting
Videos playing drums, bass, or guitar.

Finally, show little attention to
her rolling boil anger, you know

how to boil water. Don't worry, man.
This recipe is cooked all the time.

—*Timothy Gager*

LIKE FANCY PROPERTY: TANGIER #39

The floorshow at El Koutoubia Palace draws
busloads of tourists who sit in Alhambra-like
haze sipping costly drinks charmed by

this comatose rock band banging drums for
bare-bellied females wiggling tails of chiffon
some hennaed some dark none smiling

while performing a bump-grind display
oddly dull and sexless despite breasts
shaking under silk tops rather boring

going through the same routine while
guys in turbans and caftans swing swords
one spinning with a glass of water on his head

not spilling a drop echoing rhythms in
mindless mechanical perfection while
the women waggle veils between their knees

not sure who finds this fascinating except
as cultural display of retrograde humans
presenting bodies like fancy property

lead girl circling a blue flame fire-stick as
they glide off stage into silent dark looking like
products available for rental or purchase or

possible assault and if the timing's right these
female products may produce more property
birthed bloody into the numb night.

—*Nina Rubenstein Alonso*

BANDAGES

In a Russian prison, she could
hear the cries of Ukrainian men being raped.
She was pregnant. Her husband did not know.
All she wanted was her baby to be born in Ukraine.
Speaking to her stomach, urging, Wait little one.
In a prisoner exchange, her baby was born in Ukraine.

Another woman, so brutalized
She was not sure she would live,
Yet she's ready to fight again.
Still, she did not want to leave home:
Bombed out shell.
Dried blood in the dirt.
Wreckage like abstract art.
A boot in the road filled with flowers.
Someone mourning a life. Mourning their life.

In some villages, every heart stopped beating at once.
Can a village survive supported by the beating hearts of only two?
Yet the women carry on in the footprints stretched out before them.
Walking the same path,
breathing a different story for a free Ukraine

—*Gloria Mindock*

ONSET
    for J.H.K. b.11/18/1961

        I.
room's cold brightness
on all sides of me   interns   residents—
all male— a teaching hospital

pressure to push accelerates pain
reach out to one   pleading
hold my hand

his sudden surprised response *why?*
OB doctor commands *just do it*
she likes to hold hands

all childbirth is natural
unmedicated childbirth brutal
first time ever use

of my vagina as a birth canal
that moment in the cold delivery room
my life irrevocably changed

        II.
no crib   our too small apartment
on the dresser top a bassinette
courtesy of Best&Co. layette provider

mostly alone, I stand and watch her
sleeping on her back   swaddled
as the hospital nurse taught me

the size of one of my childhood dolls
the biggest one Agnes
my mother's name

but not a doll   she's breathing
what have I done
dear Lord, what have I done

how do I learn to take care of
how am I able to take care of
what I have done

—*Karen Klein*

AFFLATUS

Where are you?
I have been looking for you.
I wake up early,
into the stable,
witness Helios **sprucing** up
Aethon, Eous, Phlegon, and Pyrois.

Eos informs every dew
the chill is over,
warmth,
shining warmth is coming.

You are not there.

I listen carefully,
if Orpheus is biding behind
Eastern Phoebe, red-breasted nuthatch…
rare glimpse of their last visit…

Still not there?

Where is the lyre of Erato?
In the "*Prendi: l'anel ti dono,*"*
Bellini's La sonnambula?

And you said,
if still not found,
it could be all faded,
like Maria Callas' whispering,
"Ah! non credea mirarti
Si presto estinto, o fiore."**

Oh! Tell me not your despair.
Just watch, watch,
Selene drives her moon chariot
across the heavens.

—*Livingston Rossmoor*

Take: the ring I give you.
**"*I did not believe you would fade so soon, oh flower."*
This final aria is inscribed on Bellini's tomb in the
Catania Cathedral in Sicily.

CONVERSATION

Mind was bored one day
so he decided to play
with what it would be like
to be completely bored,
as in dead. But the rest of mind
fired up a barrage of flak,
cacophony enough
to startle heart,
who was in the midst
of an afternoon nap
What the hell was that?
yells heart.

Well, says mind, there's
this little corner of me
that's curious but, trust me,
I don't go there very often
much less stay long. That's
what we minds do, go to weird
places now and then. Sometimes
I'd rather be you—all heart,
so I don't have to think
about such things. Well,
says heart, you needn't worry.
I'm the one who should be afraid.
If I stop I won't be able to
feel ever again. I don't know
anything else—I'd be lost. Besides,
surprise!, I enjoy our arguments!
Don't you see, says mind,
that's the point. When you stop
what happens to me? I'll have
no one to play with and
I was just trying to imagine
what that might be like.
By now, mind has a headache.
Welcome to my world says heart,
I get it. If you go dead before me
what's the use of carrying on?
They have these contraptions
that keep me thumping whether
you're there or not. If you leave
I don't trust others to decide.
If you're gone, I want to go with you.
Says mind, far too morose
dear heart. Tomorrow is

tomorrow, how about
some Coltrane and a growler or two?
Heart leaps, riffs a quick jig step –
you're on, my friend!

—*Krikor Der Hohannesian*

THE NEIGHBORS

You may have seen her napping—
        flat on her couch for hours each day—
she says it stops the throbbing
    inside her head, somehow, someway.

See her through the window?
        You can't tell if she's awake.
When she gets up, she wobbles.
    Her face is pale. So what's your take?

You may have seen her walking,
      slowly, past Al's Bar, chock full
of locals back from fishing—
    their catch of bluefish, mackerel.

She tries to keep her balance
      on her walks, but you know, truth
is duller than a story
    town folk can spread. *She's on the juice.*

She slurs her words.
              Hey, no one
cares about a boring fact.
She claims her migraine throws off
  her speech and balance.
                    It's an act!

—*Paulette Demers Turco*

THE THEFT

At the Isabella Stewart Gardner Museum, Boston

I take a picture of my youngest son in profile
by a second-floor window, with Isabella's
famous nasturtiums trailing orange tiger tails
to the courtyard below, his youth thrown
into relief by timeless masterpieces. How long
until his chiseled face becomes a memory?
He has chosen this city
to start his life, the same place
where I began my own journey
so many years before—

> these streets I walked for hours.
> I used to know every crack
> in the sidewalks, the way the subway
> shrieked as it took the bend at Boylston,
> the sweep of the footbridge over the pond
> in the Public Garden, the weeping willows
> majestic, even without their leaves.

I stand before the gilded
frame in the Dutch Room —
Rembrandt's master brushstrokes in oil cut away
by the thieves' blades, green silk damask
to match the grand room's wallpaper
on display inside the empty space.
A placeholder for the return of the long-gone,
missing nearly thirty years now,
the same time I have been absent
from this city where I first learned to love.

> Now, the crowds have quadrupled, every secret
> corner populated with strangers. The Old State
> House dome still gleams gold on the hill,
> but historic cemeteries are chained closed.
> The Littlest Bar in Boston has shuttered
> its door, and The Big Dig buried
> the overhead highways I crossed under
> on the way to the waterfront.
> I used to know this place.
> But it doesn't belong to me anymore.

Before it was stolen, I stood
in front of the Vermeer on the small wooden table,

mounted like a mirror on a vanity. It was
positioned by a side window, almost
an afterthought—the intimacy of Vermeer's
home concert scene as if I had discovered
his family photo tucked in a corner.
But now the mounting is vacant. I look
into an ache that echoes.

—*Ellen Austin-Li*

ANYTHING REMEMBERED IS EVENTUALLY POETRY

Raccoons in the night were
clattering about the construction
site   knocking tools and buckets
kicking them as if to make
a racket   I rose up   leaned
on the windowsill   looked
over the fence
saw a silhouette
like a small ape running
and another following it

A light came on
in my neighbor's window
and my neighbor himself
appeared on his porch
flashlight in hand   He
muttered something loudly
as he shined his light   utter silence
tractor and saws   worker's bench
bland within his beam

One frightened animal fled
up my tree   but the others
resumed their clatter
My neighbor left a
porch light on all night

Just the sound of
rain now   such delicious
dripping and blowing   such cool
sweeps of damp wind

—*Hilary Sallick*

LAMBERTVILLE

What I loved—talking about Lambertville—
is it brought me back to my grad student days
at Princeton. The name alone—Lambertville—
rolls right off the tongue, and the Delaware there
licking the rocks—I'd scour the topos to choose
my route for a day's ride. *This is how I gained my confidence*, I say.
From Princeton, Lambertville was one of my longer rides—and New Hope—
Sue lit up when I told her I'd been where she'd just vacationed—
cool galleries, flower boxes outside the windows—
so thinking about those rides, those grad student days
what seemed to arise from out of a blank darkness
I mentioned I was molested in Lambertville once
riding my bike one sunny day—just past the footbridge
through the farm fields—grasses swaying in the breeze, sweat
beading down my face—when a hand
arrived as if I hadn't known it didn't belong
on my breast— the hand attached to a body—
a silent, grinning, smiling body—
a motorcycling body—the sun shining,
the shouting that was my mouth
working sternly, as if to say *Down boy, down*,
to show him who was Alpha, never slowing my pace
when Sue starts in—*I was running, Arboretum, lilacs
blooming*—their scent richer in early evening—
when *a baseball bat*—as she passed a monument—
a baseball bat!?—she had been running fast
so it barely glanced her head—running—
and when we finished—Lambertville—
its rough-and-tumbledness revealed—
after *Wow, same year*, and *how awful*—
how, older now, full of awe we were,
together
survivors
full of new hope.

—*Carla Schwartz*

THOSE BACKDROP CITIES

Behind the pols and infamous others
interviewed on TV, there are buildings
that resemble illuminated ladders
to Nowhere, or else rocket ships
designed for an evil Khan. Some have
rooftops that look like an MD's needles.
There is no birdspeak adoring the dawn
or driving the blue and gray skyrats
into the dark. Some of those backdrops
look like the Scandinavian Duchess,
on a cruise, sailed into a wrong left turn
and grounded on a foreign sidewalk.
There's no strand there to support
a string of wild ponies, either,
let alone enough soil for a skinny
foxglove to put down roots. Not that
I can afford it, but would I want
to live where it appears that
men in blue suits are shoveling
ragtime doubletalk at the questioners,
and the leaves withhold their oxygen
from creatures that never tell a lie?

—*Brendan Galvin*

GANG WAR

You can watch the news, a black mother crying
telling the white reporter her son is a good boy
no way involved with drugs or guns

Just the same the boy is dead, cold now as steak in
refrigerator, not dead as a door nail which never
had life, except as a nail

No, this boy walking on a sidewalk thinking about
tomorrow and the girl he will date, the basketball game
at the playground, where he is playing as if he is Kobe Bryant

Instead, as his thoughts sparkle like the stars on this
dark night the car moves slowly down the street
like a clam being steamed

Window partially open like a thought to the next world,
barrel of a pistol protrudes as a clam neck
about to excrete

The car passes the boy three shots explode like
bombs in Iraq, the car speeds off like a
NASCAR racer

Fumes cover the dead body like a shroud, blood staining
the sidewalk while in houses nearby people turn
television volume up and pull shades down

Mother cries for the reporter, for the camera,
for us as we sit on the couch with ice tea and cookies
waiting for a commercial of relief

—*Zvi A. Sesling*

THE ENGRAVER

There was the plate he scribed, cut, burred and burnished.
And there was the impression: crosswise, contrasted in ink.
He had to envision the one while cutting the other

like Cain's blood-quenching darkened to despair,
Quixote's intaglio of point and finesse
opposite the Panza bite of a burin on murky copper.

Illusion, time's lapse in the coil of a leafy vine
on a silver case, enclosing the intricate timepiece;
vapor drifts of hours to solace of form

leaving the feeling image of terror, the dragon,
under the incisive weapon of its slayer—
the stamp of the genuine obviating counterfeit.

In its shed sloughs of original wood blocks,
tin tags, granite, my uncle's engravings of rivers
refroze from seasons of understanding

for hard-soled shoes like all else obsolescing atop
our virtual ceiling—which no finger's skim can figure
from mere contour, reaching for the forge of heaven.

—Michael Todd Steffen

WRITE AN ARS POETICA

says the writing professor
in a voice earnest enough
for his assignment   he taps
a chunk of chalk on the lectern

maybe it's the caffein
he is chugging   I feel
intensity when he inquires
why do you write? for whom?

I wave my hand   insistent for instruction
but his foggy-brain remains out of focus
he torques to catch my decibels
his deaf ear refuses   he turns his back

******

I'm catapulting back to Mrs. Whiton's
second grade   standing tall   speaking clearly
*the woodpecker pecks out a little round hole
makes him a home in the telephone pole*

I'm pecking out a little round poem
of no consequence   but when mother read
slithy toves gyre-ing and gimbel-ing in the wabes
the undertow of nonsense made us guffaw

******

I am not buying a glittery Hallmark card here
nor like sitting on a wooden church pew
I am not composing a poem today
my sister makes poems   I paint signs

*everybody wants freedom   make peace not war
Black lives matter   my body my choice
take care of Mother Earth   everyone is welcome
we stand with* — so it goes decade upon decade

watch me crack out of the *silent majority*
I splash words onto butcher paper
fling my slogans across the universe
I am urgent for our children   for a future

******

I hear the professor state *time's up*
I do not know a gas leak in the air B & B
kept him tossing all night   with his lover
he rummages for his case and jacket

I grip my Ars Poetica   it reminds me
I write for all   claiming our future

—Molly Lynn Watt

sign-in sheets

there are two sign-in sheets going around
if you haven't found one do
and put your name on one before you go
no you don't have to sign both of them
if doesn't matter last name first or first name last
I don't know why there are two sign-in sheets
it says print your name why did I say sign
it doesn't matter but personnel wants it neat
what about social security numbers? uh?
you're right personnel would want
the social security number
OKAY PEOPLE
put your name and social security number
on one of these two sign-in sheets before you go I said
there are two sign-in sheets going around

—Michael Casey

THE DOG THAT RUNS THROUGH ROUGH WATERS

Because the dog won't fetch the stick
thrown in an estuary near the Black Sea
where soldiers eat oysters to forget their trench
warfare, an old man no one knows
swims out for the stick and brings it back to the dog
then walks to his picnic table
and slurps back a dish of waiting shells.

Having witnessed the old man,
and no longer concerned with anti-missile rockets
splashing debris into the ocean, the crows
watch the old-man-no-one-knows
and learn to fly backwards.

Quickly, lots of other birds notice
and stop building nests. For a time,
the soldiers go on forgetting, they ignore
everything but white wine and oysters.

Not the birds, they learn the crows' trick.
Eventually, so does a child on the beach.
She asks her father, "Do you hear that?"
"What honey?" Her father asks.

"There's nothing!"   "What'd you mean?"
"The birds, the birds have stopped…"
To humor the child the soldier looks toward the trees,

looking past the whistling teakettle-mechanism-
of-oblivion he's learned to ignore
at this distance from the front, he hears no singing.
Except for a sparrow, speaking pig Latin,
flying tail-first against the wind.

Having witnessed the birds, her father
begins walking backwards also.
Clutching his daughter's hand; for a moment,
as if she were pulling him forwards

toward crowds of people walking back
through shelled out gullies and trenches,
through half split treetops and gutted towns,
pursued by men that find no one to rape or kill
as they watch enemies retreat,
backpacks first, eyes poised down inverted sites.

When the invaders march in range of their brothers
in arms, they see the ebbing rows of troops
and fauna, and begin to walk backward also

leaving no one in the estuary full of oysters
near the Black Sea. Except the man-no-one-knows,
now older than the moon,
and the eucalyptus tree, the atlas pine,

      the yellowing ash, watching his dog swim
out in gentle waves to leave the stick floating
in estuary. Man's best friend shaking off water,
siting in sand, waiting for the old-man-

no-one-knows to retrieve the stick.
The last two beings looking at each other,
        dog walking up to man
man looking down at dog, understanding
      nothing foreign, happy even.

—*Ryan Clinesmith*

UPON READING CHRISTOPHER MARLOWE'S MASSACRE IN PARIS

Power, near absolute, needs exercise,
Quiet wisdom, a pose that will not do.
Bloody tempers hide under every guise.

With swords and daggers nobles barbarize,
Since they're able. And it must continue.
Power, near absolute, needs exercise.

The words of sleuths dim the clearest of eyes
With new suspicions, with clue after clue.
Bloody tempers hide under every guise.

One watchword, one bell, the murderous cries
From life's killing fields, only the preview.
Power, near absolute, needs exercise.

Beware of all friends, beware of all allies
Who nod, who nudge, and rivals devalue.
Bloody tempers hide under every guise.

Directed deaths their origin defies.
Kingdoms collapse. Others rise in virtue.
Power, near absolute, needs exercise.
Bloody tempers hide under every guise.

—Dennis Daly

WRITERS' BIOS—SPRING, 2023

Kathleen Aguero's most recent book of poetry is *World Happiness Index* from Tiger Bark Press. She has also co-edited three volumes of multi-cultural literature for the University of Georgia Press. She teaches in the Solstice low-residency M.F.A. program and in Changing Lives through Literature, an alternative sentencing program, and is a contributing poetry editor at *Kenyon Review*.

Nina Rubinstein Alonso's work has appeared in *The New Yorker, Ploughshares, Writing in a Woman's Voice, Peacock Journal, Broadkill Review, Wilderness House Literary Journal, Nixes Mate*, etc. Her book *This Body* was published by David Godine Press, her chapbook *Riot Wake* by Cervena Barva Press, her story collection *Distractions En Route, A Dancer's Notebook* and other stories by Ibbetson Street Press.

Michael Ansara spent many years as an activist and an organizer starting with the civil rights movement of the 1960's, going on to be a regional organizer for SDS. He spent 10 years organizing opposition to the war in Vietnam. He was for 15 years a community organizer including directing Mass Fair Share. He has worked on political campaigns, coordinated voter registration efforts, and trained many organizers. He owned and ran two successful businesses. He is the co-founder of Mass Poetry. He currently serves on the Executive Committee of the Redress Movement and the organizing team for Together We Elect. His poems have appeared in numerous journals and his essays have appeared in *Vox, Arrowsmith, Solstice* and *Cognoscenti*. His first book of poems, *What Remains*, was published in June of 2022 by Kelsay Books. He is currently working on a memoir.

Ellen Austin-Li's work has appeared in *Artemis, Thimble Literary, The Maine Review, Salamander, Rust + Moth, SWWIM,* and other places. A Best of the Net nominee, she hass published two chapbooks with Finishing Line Press: *Firefly* (2019) and *Lockdown: Scenes from Early in the Pandemic* (2021). She earned an MFA in Poetry at the Solstice Low-Residency Program. Ellen lives with her husband in Cincinnati, Ohio. Find her @www.ellenaustinli.me.

Jennifer Barber's most recent collection is *The Sliding Boat Our Bodies Made* (The Word Works, 2022). She is co-editor, with Jessica Greenbaum and Fred Marchant, of the anthology *Tree Lines: 21st Century American Poems*. Her poems have appeared recently in *On the Seawall, Mom Egg Review, Post Road,* and *32 Poems,* and are forthcoming in *Hanging Loose*. She is the current poet laureate of Brookline.

Molly Mattfield Bennett has been published in *Ibbetson Street, Constellations, Off the Coast* and *Solstice* and was nominated for the Pushcart Prize. Her first book *Name the Glory* was published by Wilderness House Press, her second *Point-No-Point* was published by FutureCycle Press. Molly is active in the Boston Poetry Community and has completed *Geography / Earth*.

Michael Brosnan is the author of two collections of poetry: *The Sovereignty of the Accidental* (Harbor Mountain Press, 2018) and *Adrift* (Grayson Books, 2023). A third book is due out in early 2024 from Broadstone Books. His poems have appeared in numerous journals. He is also the author of *Against the Current*, a book on urban education. More at www.michaelabrosnan.com.

Jessie Brown has published, in addition to two short collections, *What We Don't Know We Know* and *Lucky*, poems and translations in various local and national journals. She also collaborates in public art projects with poetry and the visual arts. She leads independent workshops for adults, both in person and online, as well as school programs in the greater Boston area (www.JessieBrown.net).

Mary Buchinger, author of six collections of poetry, including *Navigating the Reach* (Salmon Poetry, 2023), *Virology* (Lily Books, 2022), and einfühlung/*in feeling* (Main Street Rag, 2018), teaches at the Massachusetts College of Pharmacy and Health Sciences and serves on the board of the New England Poetry Club. www.MaryBuchinger.com.

Michael Casey's first book, *Obscenities,* was in the Yale poetry series in 1972. Loom Press has recently issued a new edition of his second book *Millrat*.

Ruth Chad is a psychologist who lives and works in the Boston area. Her poems have appeared in the *Aurorean, Bagels with the Bards, Connection, Psychoanalytic Couple and Family Institute of New England, Constellations, Ibbetson Street, Montreal Poems, Muddy River Poetry Review, Lily Poetry Review, Amethyst Poetry, Writing in a Woman's Voice* and *Poetry Super-Highway*. Ruth's chapbook, *The Sound of Angels*, was published by Cervena Barva Press in 2017. Her forthcoming book, *In the Absence of Birds*, will be published by Cervena Barva Press in 2024. Ruth was nominated for a Pushcart prize in 2021.

Laura Cherry is the author of the collection *Haunts* (Cooper Dillon Books) and the chapbooks *Two White Beds* (Minerva Rising) and *What We Planted* (Providence Athenaeum). She co-edited the anthology *Poem, Revised* (Marion Street Press) with Robert Hartwell Fiske, and her work has been published in journals including *The Glacier, Ekphrastic Review, Los Angeles Review, Cider Press Review*, and *DMQ Review*. She earned an MFA from the Warren Wilson Program for Writers. She works as a technical writer and lives near Boston.

Ryan Clinesmith is a poet and educator with an MFA from Hunter College. He is currently an Ed.M. candidate at the Harvard Graduate School of Education. His education related publications include the "CultureRX Field Guide", HundrED's "Implement at Scale: An Agenda for Education Innovation Implementation Research". Ryan was also the Administrative Editor in Chief of the Harvard Graduate School of Education's student run publication The Appian Way. His poetry manuscript *Epilogue to Paradise* was a finalist for the Letras Latinas-ILS/ND- Andres Montoya Poetry Prize and long listed for the C&R Press 2022 Award. His poetry can be found in the *Heavy Feather Review, Deep Overstock*, and *Indolent Books* among other publications online and in print.

Charles Coe Charles Coe is the author of four books of poetry: *All Sins Forgiven: Poems for my Parents, Picnic on the Moon, Memento Mori*, and the recently released *Purgatory Road*, all published by Leapfrog Press. He is also author of *Spin Cycles*, a novella published by Gemma Media. Charles is adjunct professor of English at Salve Regina University in Newport, Rhode Island, where he teaches in the Master of Fine Arts writing program.

Dennis Daly has published ten books of poetry and poetic translations. His most recent book is *Psalms Composed in Utter Darkness* (Dos Madres, 2023). Another book entitled *Odd Man Out* has been accepted for publication by Mad Hat Press. Penguin Random House will publish thirteen of Daly's translations in an anthology entitled *Uyghur Poems* this coming November. Please see Daly's blog site, Weights and Measures, at dennisfdaly.blogspot.com.

Sydney Doyle grew up in the mucklands near the Delaware Water Gap between New Jersey and Pennsylvania. Her poems appear in *The American Journal of Poetry, Canary, The Fourth River,* and elsewhere. She has received support from the Pennsylvania State University BA/MA program in creative writing, The Writing Seminars at Johns Hopkins University, the Sewanee Writers' Conference, and the University of Louisiana at Lafayette. She currently lives in Boston.

Timothy Gager, Number One Bestselling Author, has published 18 books of fiction and poetry, which includes his latest novel, *Joe the Salamander*. He hosted the successful Dire Literary Series in Cambridge, Massachusetts from 2001 to 2018, and started a weekly virtual series in 2020. He has had over 1000 works of fiction and poetry published, 17 nominated for the Pushcart Prize. His work also has been nominated for a Massachusetts Book Award, The Best of the Web, The Best Small Fictions Anthology and has been read on National Public Radio. In 2023, Big Table Publishing published an anthology of twenty years of his selected work, with 150 pages of new material: *The Best of Timothy Gager*.

Brendan Galvin has been seriously writing poems for the last thirty-seven years. He is currently working on his twentieth volume. His work has appeared in the *New Yorker, Poetry, Atlantic, Harper's, The New Republic, Nation, Kenyon Review, Paris Review, Georgia Review, Southern Review, Gettysburg Review, Shenandoah, Tri-Quarterly* and many others. Anthologies include *Vital Signs, Working Classics, Explore Poetry,* and *The Book of Irish-American Poetry,* among others. His prizes include The Sotheby Prize of the Avon Foundation, The Guggenheim Foundation, The First OB Hardison Prize of the Folger Shakespeare Library, the NEA and others; he was a finalist for the National Book Award.

Bridget Seley Galway artist/poet is the Arts editor/Curator of *Wilderness House Literary Review*. Her poems have been published in several magazines and anthologies. Ibbetson Press published her collection *What Moments Yield,* which is included in several library collections. Her art has been exhibited throughout New England, reviewed in several magazines, and selected for the covers of *Bagels with the Bards, Ibbetson Street,* and individual poet publications.

Harris Gardner has two poetry collections: *Chalice of Eros* co-authored with Lainie Senechal) and *No Time for Death,* published February, 2022, two chapbooks*: Lest They Become*(2003) and *Among Us (2007)* and has had 60 poems published in numerous literary journals. He has been the Poetry Editor of *Ibbetson Street* since 2010 and is co-founder of Tapestry of Voices and Boston National Poetry Month Festival with Lainie Senechal. (2001- present). He received the Ibbetson Street Life Time Achievement Award in 2015, a citation from Massachusetts House of Representatives in 2015, and the Sam Cornish Award from New England Poetry Club June 25, 2023.

Danielle Legros Georges is a creative and critical writer, translator, and the author of several books of poetry including *Maroon* (2001), *The Dear Remote Nearness of You* (2016), and *Island Heart* (2021), translations of the poems of 20th-century Haitian-French poet Ida Faubert. The former Poet Laureate of Boston, her work has been supported by fellowships and grants from institutions including The American Antiquarian Society, the PEN/Heim Translation Fund, the Boston Foundation, and the Black Metropolis Research Consortium.

Dori Hale is a longtime resident of Somerville, Massachusetts, having managed to survive gentrification. Recent poems have appeared in *Atlanta Review, Wilderness House Literary Review*, *Main Street Rag*, and *Passager*. Having published a chapbook, *Disorientation and the Weather*, in 2018, she is now working on a full-length collection, and is grateful to Gail Mazur and Frannie Lindsay for their workshops and ongoing support.

Ruth Hoberman lives in Newtonville, Massachusetts. Her poems have appeared most recently in *Connecticut River Review, RHINO, EcoTheo Review,* and *Constellations*. She retired in 2015 from the English department at Eastern Illinois University.

Andy Hoffman has published several books, and hundreds of shorter works, including fiction, biography, history, literary criticism, games, poetry, and curricula. He holds a PhD in English from Brown University and has sat on the boards of Mass Poetry and the New Media Council of the Producers Guild of America (p.g.a.). A serial entrepreneur, he has founded or cofounded several for-profit and nonprofit enterprises in educational technology. He currently lives in Brookline MA with his partner, poet Deborah Leipziger.

Richard Hoffman has published five books of poetry, *Without Paradise; Gold Star Road; Emblem; Noon until Night,* and *People Once Real*. His other books include the memoirs *Half the House* and *Love & Fury*, and the short story collection *Interference and Other Stories.*

Krikor Der Hohannesian's poems have appeared in over 275 literary journals including *The South Carolina Review, Atlanta Review, Louisiana Literature, Connecticut Review, Comstock Review* and *Natural Bridge*. He is a five-time Pushcart Prize nominee and author of three books, *Ghosts and Whispers* (Finishing Line Press, 2010), *Refuge in the Shadows* (Cervena Barva Press, 2013) and *First Generation* (Dos Madres Press, 2020). *Ghosts and Whispers"* was a finalist for the Massachusetts Book Awards poetry category in 2011. *First Generation* was selected as a "must read" by Massachusetts Book Awards in 2021.

Tom Holmes founded *Redactions: Poetry & Poetics* twenty years ago. He is also the author of five full-length collections of poetry, including *The Book of Incurable Dreams* (forthcoming from Xavier Review Press) and *The Cave*, which won The Bitter Oleander Press Library of Poetry Book Award for 2013, as well as four chapbooks. He teaches at Nashville State Community College (Clarksville)

Madeleine Fuchs Holzer is Educator in Residence at the Academy of American Poets. In this capacity, she is presently curating an anthology of *Teach this Poem* lessons, many of which she wrote over the past ten years. "My Sofa Becomes a Time Machine" is the first poem she has published in almost 30 years. Earlier poetry appeared in *Pearl, The Patterson Literary Review* and other literary magazines. A former resident at MacDowell, she lives in Cambridge, Massachusetts.

Ruth Holzer is the author of eight chapbooks, most recently *Home and Away* (dancing girl press) and *Living in Laconia* (Gyroscope Press). Her poems have appeared in *Southern Poetry Review, Blue Unicorn, Slant, Poet Lore* and *Freshwater* among other journals and anthologies. She has received several Pushcart Prize nominations.

Stephen M. Honig has published five volumes of poetry, most recently *Burn-Out,* and a collection of short stories entitled *Noir Ain't the Half of It*. His novel, *The Event,* is to be published this Fall. A practicing corporate attorney and member of the Board of Directors of New England Poetry Club, Steve resides in Newton, Massachusetts with his wife, youngest son and recalcitrant dog Popcorn.

Justin Hunt grew up in rural Kansas and lives in Charlotte, NC. Fluent in German and Spanish, Hunt has won several awards, most recently 1st place in the Porter Fleming Literary Competition, 2nd place in the River Styx and Strokestown (Ireland) international contests, and commendations in numerous other competitions, including those conducted by *New Ohio Review, New Letters,* The Munster Literature Centre (Ireland), The Bridport Arts Centre (U.K.), and Robinson Jeffers Tor House. Hunt's work also appears in *Barrow Street, Five Points, Michigan Quarterly Review, American Literary Review,* and *Nimrod,* among others. For more information on Justin, please visit justinhunt.online.

Robert K. Johnson, now retired, was a Professor of English who taught at Suffolk University for many years. For eight years, he was also Poetry Editor of *Ibbetson Street* magazine. His poems have been published in a wide variety of magazines here and abroad. The most recent collections of his poems are *From Mist to Shadow* and *Choir Of Day.*

Lawrence Kessenich has written poetry, plays, novels, screenplays, and essays. He won the 2010 Strokestown International Poetry Prize, and his poetry has been published in *Sewanee Review, Atlanta Review, Poetry Ireland Review,* and many other magazines. Three of his poems were read on NPR's *The Writer's* Almanac and three nominated for the Pushcart Prize. He has published two chapbooks, *Strange News* and *Pearl,* and two full-length books, *Before Whose Glory* and *Age of Wonders,* and *Hard Times Require Furious Dancing* will be available soon. He has also published a novel, *Cinnamon Girl,* and his plays have been performed in several states. All of his books are available at lawrence-writer.com.

For **Karen Klein**, writing poems and performing contemporary modern dance constitute her creative activity. Her first poetry book, *This Close* (Ibbetson Press) was published in 2022. She has completed a chapbook set of poems on living fully in a female body. Her current project is a long poem on David, King of Israel, which will structure a performance by a male dancer with original music.

Ted Kooser's most recent collection of poems is *Cotton Candy: Poems Dipped Out of the Air*, from University of Nebraska Press. Kooser is a former U S Poet Laureate and winner of the Pulitzer Prize. He is a long time contributor to Ibbetson Street.

Deborah Leipziger is an author, poet, and advisor on sustainability. Born in Brazil, Ms. Leipziger is the author of several books on sustainability and human rights. Her poems have been published in eight countries, in such magazines and journals as *Pangyrus,Salamander, Lily Poetry Review,* and *Revista Cardenal.* She is the co-founder of Soul-Lit, an on-line poetry magazine. Her new collection of poems, *Story & Bone,* was published in early 2023 by Lily Poetry Review Books. Her chapbook, *Flower Map,* was published by Finishing Line Press. Her work appears in numerous anthologies, including *Tree Lines: 21st Century American Poems.*

Ellaraine Lockie's recent poems won Oprelle Publishing's Masters Contest and their Bigger Than Me Contest, Poetry Super Highway Contest, Nebraska Writers Guild's Women of the Fur Trade Poetry Contest and *New Millennium's* Monthly Musepaper Poetry Contest. Ellaraine teaches poetry workshops and serves as Poetry Editor for the lifestyles magazine LILIPOH.

Jacquelyn Malone's work has appeared in *Poetry, Beloit Poetry Journal, Cimarron Review, Cortland Review, Poetry Northwest,* and many other publications. Poems published in the *Beloit Poetry Journal* and *Ibbetson Street* have been nominated for the Pushcart Prize. Her chapbook, *All Waters Run to Lethe,* was published by Finishing Line Press. She recently won the Tupelo Press Broadside contest.

Eileen McCluskey's poetry has appeared in *Main Street Rag*, on WBUR's Radio Boston, in *Rufous City Review, Ibbetson Street, 6S, Haiku Journal, Boston College Magazine,* and other publications. Eileen has several micro chapbooks with Origami Poems Project, including the popular *Divorce Haiku.* Her chapbook, *Topless,* was published by Main Street Rag. Eileen was among the poets included in the Wickford Art Association's 2019 collaborative reading and exhibit with poets and painters. She was an invited reader at the 2021 and 2022 Watertown Arts Festivals, and was a finalist in The Poetry Loft 2015 Chapbook Contest, and in the Cambridge Poetry Awards 2012 competition.

Susan Lloyd McGarry has published poetry in small magazines and given readings and workshops in London and Oregon, as well as in the Boston area. Her poems have been anthologized in *The Poetry of Peace* and *Beyond Raised Voices.* Named Bard of the Boston Irish Festival for her poem, "Memory of Coumeenole,"she read there to 1000+ people. Until recently she wrote newsletters and ran social media for a center devoted to health and human rights. Previously as managing editor of the *Harvard Divinity Bulletin*, she edited their poetry issue, *The Radiant Imagination.* She now freelances on a limited basis.

Triona McMorrow lives in Dunlaoghaire, County Dublin. She was shortlisted for The International Francis Ledwidge Poetry Competition in 2009, 2011 and 2016 and The Galway University Hospitals Arts Trust poetry competition in 2013. She has been published by *Cyphers* and *North West Words* and has had several poems published in *Ibbetson Street*. She has five poems published in the anthology *Bealtaine* (2014). She has a poem in *Washing Windows Too*, a recent anthology of women poets published by Arlen House (2022).

Gary Metras's poems have appeared in such periodicals as *America, The Common, Ibbetson Street, Poetry,* and *Poetry East.* His newest of eight books of poems, *Vanishing Points* (Dos Madres Press, 2021), was selected as a 2022 Must Read Poetry Title in the Massachusetts Books of the Year Program. His new book, *Marble Dust,* is due from Cervena Barva Press. A retired educator, he fly fishes the streams and rivers of western Massachusetts as often as possible.

David P. Miller's collection, *Bend in the Stair*, was published by Lily Poetry Review Books in 2021. *Sprawled Asleep* was published by Nixes Mate Books in 2019. His poems have appeared in *Meat for Tea, Solstice, Kestrel, Paterson Literary Review, subTerrain, Constellations, Jerry Jazz Musician, museum of americana, Last Stanza,* and *LEON Literary Review*, among others, as well as several anthologies.

Gloria Mindock is editor of Červená Barva Press. She is the author of 6 poetry collections and 3 chapbooks. Her poems have been published and translated into eleven languages. Her recent book is *ASH* (Glass Lyre Press, 2021) won 7 book awards and was translated into Serbian by Milutin Durickovic and published by Alma Press. Gloria was the Poet Laureate in Somerville, Massachusetts in 2017 and 2018. www.gloriamindock.com

Paula Reed Nancarrow (she/her) is a poet, a Pushcart Prize- and Best of the Net- nominee, and winner of the Winter 2020 *Sixfold* Poetry Prize. She grew up in the Southern Tier of New York State and now calls Minnesota home. Recent poems have appeared in *Nixes Mate, Plainsongs, The Southern Review, Cider Press Review, The Madrigal, and Halfway Down the Stairs*. Find her at paulareednancarrow.com.

Tomas O'Leary has taught literature, creative writing, and Spanish at the college, high school and elementary levels. For over 20 years he has worked as an expressive therapist with Alzheimer's groups, conversing, singing, playing accordion. His full-length volumes of poetry are *Fool at the Funeral, The Devil Take a Crooked House,* and *In the Wellspring of the Ear* (all from Lynx House Press), and *A Prayer for Everyone* (from Ilora Press).

Chad Parenteau hosts Boston's long-running Stone Soup Poetry series. His latest collection is *The Collapsed Bookshelf.* His poetry has appeared in journals such as *Résonancee, Molecule, Pocket Lint, Cape Cod Poetry Review, Tell-Tale Inklings, Off The Coast, The Skinny Poetry Journal, The New Verse News, Nixes Mate Review* and anthologies such as *French Connections* and *Reimagine America.* He serves as Associate Editor of the online journal *Oddball Magazine.*

Marge Piercy has published 20 poetry collections, most recently *On the Way Out, Turn Off the Light* (Knopf) and 17 novels, including *Sex Wars*. PM Press reissued *Vida* and *Dance The Eagle to Sleep* and brought out the short story collections *The Cost of Lunch, Etc.* and *My Body My Life* (essays and poems). Her most recent novel is *Sex Wars*. She has read at more than 575 venues here and abroad.

Denise Provost has published in various journals. She received the Maria C. Faust Sonnet Competition Best Love Sonnet award in 2012, and the New England Poetry Club's Samuel Washington Allen Prize in 2021. Provost has published two poetry collections: *Curious Peach* (2019) and *City of Stories* (2021.) She was elected co-president of the New England Poetry Club in 2022.

Gayle Roby's work has appeared in several journals, including *The Iowa Review, The Ohio Review, Prairie Schooner,* and *Ibbetson Street.* She received an MFA in poetry from Warren Wilson College. Before retiring from Bunker Hill Community College, she taught English to speakers of other languages. She was born and grew up in downstate Illinois. A Quaker, she lives in Arlington with her family and cats..

Elizabeth A. Rodgers is a poet and lawyer of Watertown Massachusetts, who helped form the Watertown Literary Squad, performing poetry at their Arts Market in 2021 and 2022. She has read poetry at Wellesley College, a National Employment Lawyers' Convention, and at Cambridge coffee houses. She recently discovered her Higgins ancestors were poets. She thanks Lit Squadroons, Dewitt Henry, Kathleen Spivack, Lawrence Kessenich, Pia Owens, Ricardo Calleja, Patrick Fairbairn, and Marjory Greenberg.

Livingston Rossmoor has written and published 20 poetry books. His poems have been published in numerous publications: *The Lyric, Ibbetson Street, Poetry Quarterly, California Quarterly* (California State Poetry Society), *Wisconsin Review, Main Street Rag, Rosebud* literary magazine, *Time of Singing* poetry journal, *Chronogram* magazine, *Loch Raven Review and Glimpse* poetry magazine.

Hilary Sallick is the author of *Love Is A Shore* (forthcoming from Lily Poetry Review Books), *Asking the Form* (Cervena Barva Press, 2020) and *Winter Roses* (Finishing Line Press, 2017). Her work appears regularly in *Ibbetson Street*, and in other journals such as *Vita Poetica, Leon Literary Review, Poetry Porch*, and *Constellations*. She's a board member of the New England Poetry Club and a teacher in Somerville, Massachusetts.

Carla Schwartz's poems have been widely published, including in *The Practicing Poet* (Diane Lockward, Ed) and in her collections *Signs of Marriage, Mother, One More Thing,* and *Intimacy with the Wind.* Her CB99videos (https://www.youtube.com/user/cb99videos) has 2,400,000+ views. Learn more at carlapoet.comor or_@cb99videos on social. Recent publications and acceptances include *The Ear, Channel, California Quarterly, Cutthroat, Inquisitive Eater, Paterson Literary Review, Triggerfish, The MacGuffin, Verse-Virtual,* and *Leon*. Carla Schwartz is a 2023 recipient of a Massachusetts Cultural Council Grant.

Lainie Senechal, poet, artist, and former Poet Laureate of Amesbury, MA lives in Peterborough, NH. She was Poet-in-Residence at Mass Audubon's Joppa Flats Education Center. She has read and featured at many venues throughout New England. Her poetry has appeared in various journals and four anthologies. She co-authored two volumes of poetry. Her chapbook is *Vocabulary of Awakening,* published by Pudding House Press.

Zvi A. Sesling, , Brookline, MA Poet Laureate (2017-2020), is a five-time Puschcart Prize nominee He has published poems and flash fiction. He edits *Muddy River Poetry Review* and *10By10 Flash Fiction Stories.* He published four poetry books and three poetry chapbooks and a flash fiction chapbook. His latest flash fiction is *Secret Behind the Gate* from Cervena Barva Press.. He lives in Brookline, MA with his wife Susan J. Dechter.

Wendell Smith is a retired physician who lives in Melrose. His poetry has appeared in *The Kansas Quarterly, Constellation, View Northwest, Ibbetson Street, Muddy River Poetry Review, The Lyric* and elsewhere. He thinks Ramon Guthrie's *Maximum Security Ward* should be to 20th century poetry what Moby Dick is to 19th century fiction. If he were in the last chapter of *Fahrenheit* 451, where people memorize literature to save it, he would memorize Guthrie.

Michael Todd Steffen is the recipient of a Massachusetts Cultural Council Fellowship and an Ibbetson Street Press Poetry Award. His poems have appeared in journals including *The Boston Globe, E-Verse Radio, The Lyric, The Dark Horse*, and *The Poetry Porch*. Of his second book, *On Earth As It Is*, now available from Cervena Barva Press, Joan Houlihan has noted *Steffen's intimate portraits, sense of history, surprising wit and the play of dark and light…the striking combination of the everyday and the transcendent.*

Sandra Thaxter lives in Newburyport Massachusetts. She was born in Portland, Maine. She studied poetry and writing in New York city and is currently studying with Alfred Nicol and Rhina Espaillat of the Powow Poets. Published Chapbooks by Finishing Line Press: *The Colors of Water the Shapes of* Stone and *Illuminated*.

Jeff Tigchelaar is the author of *Certain Streets at an Uncertain Hour* (Woodley Press), winner of the Kansas Authors Club Nelson Poetry Book Award. *Prayed On at the Y* (7 Kitchens Press) and *Love & Wrestling* (Ravenna Press), both chapbooks, were published in 2022. His poems appear in *Beloit Poetry Journal* (as runner-up for the Adrienne Rich Prize), *New Ohio Review, AGNI, Pleiades*, and *North American Review*, as well as in *Best New Poets* and *New Poetry from the Midwest*.

Keith Tornheim, a biochemistry professor at Boston University School of Medicine, has six recent books, *The Sacrifice of Isaac*; *I Am Lilith, Dancer on the Wind*; *Spirit Boat: Poems of Crossing Over*; *Can You Say Kaddish for the Living?*; *Fireflies*; *Spoiled Fruit: Adam and Eve in Eden and Beyond.* His poems have appeared in *Ibbetson Street, The Somerville Times, Boston Literary Magazine, Muddy River Poetry Review* and *Poetica*.

Bill Tremblay is a poet. novelist, essayist and reviewer. He has nine books of poetry including *Crying in the Cheap Seats, Duhamel: Ideas of Order in Little Canada, Shooting Script: Door of Fire, and Walks Along the Ditch*. His latest book is entitled *The Quinebaug at Twelve*, which is looking for a publisher. Poems from that book have been published in *Resonance, Worcester Review, Re-Dactions, Cimarron Reivew, Lummox, Hamilton Stone Review, Caesura,* and *Ginosko Literary Journal*. His work has been featured in many anthologies, including Pushcart Prize, *Best American Poetry*, and *Poets of the New American West,* and *The Jazz Anthology*.

Paulette Demers Turco's recent book *Shimmer* (Kelsay Books, April, 2023) is an ekphrastic collection of her art and poetry. A Powow River Poet since 2018, she is editor of *The Powow River Poets Anthology II* (Able Muse Press, 2021) and co-organizer of Powow Poetry readings. Her chapbook *In Silence* (Finishing Line Press) was released in 2018. Her poetry appears in *The Lyric, Ibbetson Street, The Poetry Porch, Mezzo Cammin, Loch Raven Review, Quill & Parchment* (and art), and others. Awards include the Robert Frost Poetry Award.

Molly Lynn Watt is a poet, playwright, educator, activist for social justice and a healthy planet. She has published widely, including in *Shadow People, Ibbetson Street, On Wings of Song, Consider This*, chapbook, educational alternatives and on film. *George and Ruth: Songs and Letters of the Spanish Civil War*, with Dan Lynn Watt, was published through Educational Alternatives, Teaching with Logo, Addison Wesley and reissued through Constructing Modern Knowledge. Molly lives in cohousing & plays ukulele.

Printed in the USA
CPSIA information can be obtained
at www.ICGtesting.com
LVHW090755190923
758538LV00016B/1489